Cookies

M. Dalton King

with Kathy Blake and Juliet M. Rogers

MetroBooks

MetroBooks

An Imprint of Friedman/Fairfax Publishers

Library of Congress Cataloging-in-Publication Data

King, M. Dalton.
    Cookies / M. Dalton King, with Kathy Blake, and Juliet M. Rogers.
        p. cm.
    ISBN 1-58663-047-4 (alk. paper)
    1. Cookies. 2. Holiday cookery. I. Blake, Kathy. II. Rogers, Juliet M. III. Title.

TX772 .K57 2000
641.8'654—dc21

                                                                00-038026

Editors: Betsy Beier and Ann Kirby-Payne
Art Director: Jeff Batzli
Designer: Jennifer Markson
Photography Director: Christopher Bain
Production Manager: Maria Gonzalez

Color separations by Fine Arts, Pte.
Printed in Hong Kong by Midas Printing Limited
10 9 8 7 6 5 4 3 2 1

For bulk purchases and special sales, please contact:
Friedman/Fairfax Publishers
Attention: Sales Department
15 West 26th Street
New York, NY 10010
212/685-6610 FAX 212/685-1307

Visit our website:
www.metrobooks.com

CONTENTS

Introduction
∞ 4 ∞

The Basics
∞ 4 ∞

The Recipes
∞ 9 ∞

INTRODUCTION

In a world filled with cakes, pies, pastries, ice cream, and candy, cookies have managed to maintain a place in our sweet-eating hearts that is strictly their own. All the ingredients that go into making those others can be, and often are, used to make cookies, but cookies have a versatility that, one can say without exaggeration, extends far beyond that of the other sweets.

Amazingly flexible, cookies come in a rainbow of different tastes and textures. Butter, sugar, nuts, chocolate, espresso, candies, fruits, jams, jellies, and peanut butter are just a few of the countless ingredients that have found their way into the mixing bowl. Adjustable to any hand size, cookies can be eaten on the run or, in a more formal setting, on plates accompanied by cups of tea or coffee. Cookies are at home in a variety of settings: in decorative jars, picnic baskets, packed in brown bags with sandwiches, or hanging on Christmas trees. Cookies are suitable for any occasion and can fit almost any bill of fare.

All of the recipes in this book are perfect for the holidays, and most of them are perfect all year round. And, to help you produce excellent cookies every time, a chapter called *The Basics* provides a wealth of useful information—from advice on technique, equipment, and ingredients to hints for freezing and storing your tasty treats.

So whatever the occasion, begin baking early. With a freezer and pantry filled with goodies, you'll be able to bring your homemade cookies to neighborhood potluck parties or bake sales. Naturally, you'll want some cookies to share with family and friends on all the special occasions of the year. Children will be dazzled by fancifully decorated gingerbread people, and adults will enjoy buttery spritz cookies and delectable Mexican sugar cookies. And you, the baker, will be blessed with the fun of planning and baking, as well as the satisfaction of eating and giving away plenty of beautiful, delicious cookies.

THE BASICS

Baking wonderful cookies takes organization more than skill, for with a little practice, skill can be acquired. Before starting any recipe it is always wise to read it through completely once, or even twice. Make sure you have all the

necessary ingredients, equipment, and perhaps most importantly, enough time and space to do the job properly. It has been my experience that mistakes generally happen when you're rushed, find out at the last minute that you're missing a key ingredient, or are so cramped for work space that everything becomes chaotic. The time and space are up to you, the rest I can help you with.

Equipment

It doesn't take, nor is it necessary, to have a lot of equipment to make cookies. A mixing bowl, spoon, cookie sheet, spatula, and a smooth glass for rolling and cutting will get you by. But why not, if you have the inclination, make it easy on yourself?

It only takes a quick trip through the kitchen section of any housewares store for one to become apprised of the variety of baking equipment available to the modern baker. Baking sheets come in in cast iron, aluminum, and stainless steel. They can be insulated, Teflon-coated, light- or heavy- duty professional strength, with or without sides. All work. Each has points in its favor.

I find both a food processor and mixer to be invaluable kitchen aids. Between the two you'll find there isn't anything you can't mix, chop, or blend. And it's certainly easier to make cookie dough with a mixer than a spoon.

Additionally several bowls of assorted sizes, and three or four pans, again of various sizes, will do. Other helpful basics include metal and rubber spatulas, several sizes of round and shaped cookie cutters, a rolling pin, and a pastry brush. Some recipes in this book use a cookie press and pastry bag. Beyond that, it's up to you whether you wish to equip your kitchen with cookie irons, molds, and any other cookie-making devices that are currently on the market. Whatever you choose, the tips listed below may prove a useful guide.

✳ Dark, nonstick cookie sheets are easy to use and clean because they usually don't have to be greased or floured (although when parchment paper is suggested it is wise to follow that advice). However, nonstick pans have a tendency to cook hotter and therefore brown cookies faster. When using such pans, lower the suggested oven temperature by 25°, and remember to use a plastic spatula on nonstick pans to prevent scratches or rips in the pan's coating.

✳ Insulated or cushioned baking sheets protect cookies from baking too quickly or browning too fast. But this means that your cookies may take longer to bake; you'll have to adjust the baking time, leaving the cookies in the oven a little longer. Check them every 2 to 3 minutes after you've passed the suggested baking time.

✳ Heavy, professional, cast-iron pans are well balanced and won't buckle. But they may bake your cookies in less time than is suggested. When in doubt, check your cookies every 2 to 3 minutes after they have baked for 5.

✳ One-sided cookie sheets make moving cookies from pan to rack a breeze. But the other side of the coin is if the pan is bumped or jiggled, your cookies may slide off when you don't want them to, so be careful.

✳ If you plan to bake a lot of brownies, blondies, or bars, an investment in a 13x9-inch pan plus an 8-inch or 9- inch square pan should cover your needs. When an exact pan size is recommended, particularly for bar-type cookies, it's best follow that recommendation. A pan that is too large will most likely result in an overbaked product, while too small a pan will produce the reverse.

✳ A wide-mouth spatula is a helpful cookie utensil. It works equally well for large or small cookies, sometimes enabling you to scoop up two small cookies at a time.

✳ A narrow (1- to 1 ¹/₂- inch) pastry brush works best for cookies, allowing you to cover the cookies efficiently without dripping anything onto the pan.

✳ Rolling pins can be wood or metal, heavy or light, long or short. Opt for comfort. Choose the one that feels best in your hands and is easiest to use.

✳ Cookie scoops are a great help when baking dropped cookies. They provide a uniform shape and size and are convenient and easy to use and clean. Leveled off on the side of the bowl, a scoop holds 1 tablespoon of dough.

✳ One or two sets of measuring spoons, metal or plastic, are a must for any baker.

Ingredients

When it comes to baking, what goes into your dough will invariably affect the final product. Using quality ingredients and knowing how and when substitutions can be made is a key to making successful cookies.

✳ In most recipes, butter and margarine can be used interchangeably. However, it's best not to substitute diet, light, or whipped butter for traditional whole milk sticks. The fat content of a recipe is important and is often the deciding factor between a great cookie and a not-so-great one.

✳ Make sure your butter is fresh before putting it into a dough. Although the risk of spoilage is low, if the butter has been sitting out for a period of time (12 to 24 hours), it may have gone bad so it's best to check.

✳ Shortening sticks are convenient to use, easily stored, and eliminate the need to clean measuring cups.

✳ Milk chocolate and semisweet chocolate can be used interchangeably, according to taste. For a slightly sharper taste, substitute bittersweet chocolate for semisweet chocolate squares.

✳ Pouches of pre-melted chocolate are a marvelous help and can be mixed directly into a batter or dough—eliminating altogether a tiresome step and cleanup.

✳ You can use granulated sugar when a recipe call for superfine. (Superfine sugar does however give the dough a finer texture.)

Techniques

Cookies are usually classified according to method of preparation or type of cookie—they can be rolled and cut, dropped, sliced, pressed, hand formed into balls and other shapes, or spread into pans and cut into bars. Whatever the shape of a cookie (flat, round, or bar) the methods and techniques enlisted to successfully bake them are the same. You'll find helpful suggestions and recommendations listed below.

✳ Rather than adding more flour to stiffen up a too-soft dough, refrigerate it, covered, for at least an hour, and longer if necessary.

✳ If you're working with a butter dough in a hot kitchen, you may find it helpful to refrigerate it between steps, which prevents the butter in the dough from becoming too warm.

✳ When using a mixer or food processor to make a recipe calling for coarsely chopped or whole nuts, pieces of candy, chocolate chips, or fruit, mix the dough with the machine just up to the point where you add in the chunks; finish mixing it by hand.

✳ You'll find that rolling dough is facilitated by flouring both your surface and rolling pin. It is also beneficial to lightly flour the tips of utensils such as knives and cookie cutters, as well as your hands and fingers if the dough requires a lot of handling.

✳ Press lightly but firmly when using a rolling pin. Too heavy a push will tear the dough. You'll find it helps to roll from the center outward in all four directions.

✳ The thinner you roll the dough, the crisper the cookie will be.

✳ Press down firmly on cookie cutters to ensure a clean cut.

✳ Cut your cookies out as closely together as possible to eliminate using the trimmings over and over.

✳ When a recipe calls for forming the dough into rolls or logs and refrigerating, give the rolls a turn from time to time as they chill to prevent flat surfaces from forming.

- When a greased pan is called for, cooking sprays can be just as effective as buttering, greasing, and flouring, but are more convenient to use and easier to clean up.
- Parchment paper is a nonstick paper used to line baking pans. It is particularly effective when baking cookies with jams or chocolate. I use a sheet several times over. If it becomes messy I give it a shake or turn it over.
- Preheat the oven to the suggested temperature for a minimum of 15 minutes before beginning to bake.
- To prevent cookies from running together and attaching to each other while baking, leave 1 inch of space between rolled cookies and 2 inches between dropped or butter ones.
- Dropped and butter cookies spread very easily, so it is especially important that pans are allowed to cool before reusing them.
- You'll save time and energy if you have two pans going at once: one in the oven with cookies baking, and the second (after it's cooled) being prepared with the next batch.
- Baking cookies in a humid climate may yield less than perfect results. High humidity will take the crisp right out of your cookie.
- Cut bar cookies, blondies, and brownies only after they have cooled completely to get a clean cut rather than a jagged edge.
- Cooling cookies in a single layer allows the air to circulate around them for better cooling, and prevents a soggy or marred product.

Storing Cookies

Of course, part of the fun of baking cookies is having tons of them on hand for parties or to ship to far-off friends and family. Baking ahead is the best way to have a wide variety of cookies available for loved ones and guests. If you're planning to ship cookies, there are several tricks that will ensure a safe trip for your sweet surprises.

- As a rule, it is best to store soft cookies, bars, and brownies in tightly covered containers. They will retain their moisture and remain soft and chewy.
- A small slice of apple packed into the same container as soft cookies will keep them moist and chewy.
- Crisp cookies will keep their crunch if stored in loosely covered containers where the air is able to circulate around them.
- To maintain maximum flavor and texture, store different types of cookies in separate containers.
- If you are shipping cookies, choose cookies that are strong enough to arrive whole, and will stay fresh during the trip. The best cookies for mailing are firm, but not brittle; crisp, but not delicate.
- Glazed cookies travel well, but don't send cookies with soft frostings.

THE
RECIPES

Stained Glass Windows

Clear candies melted into different shapes give these cookies the look of stained glass. Instead of using cookie cutters, you can also create original cookie designs by rolling the dough into long ropes, and molding them into different shapes.

1^1/$_3$ cups butter	1^1/$_4$ teaspoons nutmeg
1^1/$_3$ cups sugar	5^1/$_4$ cups flour
^{1}/$_2$ cup milk	Clear hard candies, sorted by color and crushed
4 eggs, well beaten	

Cream together butter and sugar. Beat milk together with eggs and add to butter mixture. Add nutmeg to flour, and then mix gradually into butter mixture. Wrap in waxed paper and chill for 1 hour.

Preheat oven to 350°F. Cover baking sheets with foil.

Roll dough ^{1}/$_4$ inch thick and cut out with large cookie cutters of your choice. From the center of each cookie, cut out a smaller shape using a smaller cookie cutter, making sure to leave at least ^{1}/$_4$ inch of edge around the center hole. Place cookies on a prepared baking sheet. Fill centers with crushed candy, one color to a hole. If you are planning to use the cookies as ornaments, use a drinking straw to cut a hole through the top of each cookie (through which you'll be able to pass a loop of string).

Bake 6 to 9 minutes, or until the candy melts. Cool 5 minutes to solidify candy before moving the cookies carefully to wire racks.

MAKES ABOUT 5 DOZEN COOKIES

Peanut Butter & Chocolate Swirls

"Red Hots" are cinnamon-flavored candies. Placed in the center of each swirl they provide an unusual taste dimension, something akin to eating sorbet at the end of a meal. You can find these fiery red buttons in grocery, candy, and large drug stores.

Peanut butter dough

1/2 cup unsalted butter at room temperature

1/2 cup creamy peanut butter

1/2 cup packed dark brown sugar

1 teaspoon vanilla

1 1/2 cups all-purpose flour

1 1/2 teaspoons baking powder

Chocolate dough

1/2 cup unsalted butter at room temperature

1/2 cup granulated sugar

1 egg yolk

2 ounces unsweetened chocolate, melted and cooled to room temperature

1/2 teaspoon vanilla

1 1/2 cups all-purpose flour

1/4 cup unsweetened cocoa

1 1/2 teaspoons baking powder

1 box Red Hots for decoration

For the peanut butter dough, cream butter, peanut butter, and sugar until light and fluffy. Blend in the vanilla. Sift together flour and baking powder and add to the creamed butter mixture, mixing until a dough is formed. Wrap dough in wax paper or plastic wrap. Chill for at least 1 hour but not more than 2 hours.

For the chocolate dough, cream butter and sugar until light and fluffy. Beat in egg yolk, chocolate, and vanilla. Sift together flour, cocoa, and baking powder and add to the creamed butter mixture, mixing until a dough is formed. Wrap dough in wax paper or plastic wrap. Chill for at least 1 hour but not more than 2 hours.

Unwrap the two doughs and divide each in half. Place half the chocolate dough on a sheet of floured wax paper and gently roll into a 12x7-inch rectangle. Leave the dough on the wax paper and set aside. Using a fresh sheet, repeat this process with half the peanut butter dough.

Carefully flip the chocolate rectangle on top of the peanut butter rectangle. Using the wax paper as a guide, roll the 12-inch length into a tight tube. Wrap in fresh wax paper and chill overnight. Repeat this process with the remaining dough.

Preheat oven to 375°F.

Unwrap the rolls one at a time, and cut $^1/_2$-inch slices out of the rolls. Place the slices 1 to 1$^1/_2$ inches apart on a greased baking sheet and place a Red Hot in the center of each cookie. Bake 12 to 15 minutes, or until the cookies are lightly browned. Remove cookies from oven and allow them to remain on baking sheet for 5 minutes, then place on racks to finish cooling.

MAKES 3 TO 4 DOZEN
COOKIES

Zoo Cookies

These crisp, slightly lemony cookies cut in the shape of animals are a favorite with both adults and children. Make these animal shapes with cookie cutters, available at most specialty cooking stores.

$^1/_2$ cup unsalted butter

$^1/_2$ cup shortening

$^2/_3$ cup granulated sugar

$^1/_3$ cup packed light brown sugar

1 egg

1 teaspoon vanilla

2 tablespoons fresh lemon juice

1 tablespoon finely grated lemon zest

$2^1/_2$ cups all-purpose flour

1 tablespoon baking powder

$^1/_4$ teaspoon salt

1 egg white mixed with 1 tablespoon water

Colored sugar crystals (can be found in most grocery stores or specialty shops)

Preheat oven to 375°F. Lightly coat baking sheets with cooking spray.

In a mixing bowl, cream the butter, shortening, and sugars until light and fluffy. Beat in the egg. Blend in the vanilla, lemon juice, and zest. Sift together the flour, baking powder, and salt. Add the dry ingredients to the mixing bowl in two parts, mixing after each addition. Mix well until a dough is formed.

Place a third of the dough on a well-floured surface and roll out $^1/_4$ inch thick. Cut out cookies with the cutters and carefully place 1 inch apart on a prepared baking sheet. Using a pastry brush, "paint" the top of each cookie with the egg white mixture. Sprinkle colored sugar crystals over the top of each cookie. Place the cookie sheet in the oven and bake 12 to 15 minutes, or until cookies are lightly browned. Remove from oven and cool on racks. Repeat this process with the remaining dough.

MAKES 3½ TO 4 DOZEN COOKIES

Gingerbread People

Gather the children to help make and decorate these fun Christmas cookies.

$^1/_2$ cup butter or margarine, softened
1 cup packed light brown sugar
$1^1/_2$ cups light molasses
$^2/_3$ cup water
$6^1/_2$ cups all-purpose flour
2 teaspoons baking soda
2 teaspoons salt

2 teaspoons ground ginger
1 teaspoon ground cinnamon
1 teaspoon allspice
$^1/_2$ teaspoon cloves
   Raisins, semisweet chocolate pieces, colored sprinkles, sugar, and/or nuts, for decorating

In a large bowl, beat butter or margarine and sugar until creamy. Add the molasses and beat until blended, then mix in the water. In another large bowl, stir together flour, baking soda, salt, ginger, cinnamon, allspice, and cloves. Gradually beat dry mixture into butter mixture until dough is stiff and blended together. Divide the dough into quarters. Cover and refrigerate for at least 4 hours.

Preheat the oven to 350°F. Lightly grease baking sheets.

Roll dough $^1/_4$ inch thick. Cut out cookies with people-shaped cookie cutters. Transfer to a baking sheet. Press raisins, chocolate pieces, sprinkles, sugar, and/or nuts into place before baking.

Bake 10 to 12 minutes, or until lightly browned. Remove to wire racks and cool completely.

Cookies may be further decorated with piped icing: Mix together 2 cups sifted confectioners' sugar and 2 to 3 tablespoons milk or light cream to make an icing of piping consistency.

MAKES ABOUT 4 DOZEN COOKIES

Judie's Wine Stars

A touch of sherry or port makes this a perfect cookie for the grownups on your list.

$^1/_2$ cup unsalted butter, at room temperature

$1^1/_2$ cups packed light brown sugar

1 large egg

$^1/_2$ cup finely chopped blanched almonds

$2^1/_2$ cups all-purpose flour

$^3/_4$ teaspoon cinnamon

$^1/_2$ teaspoon baking soda

3 tablespoons sherry or port

$^1/_8$ teaspoon almond extract

Preheat oven to 400°F. Lightly spray baking sheets with cooking spray.

Cream butter and sugar together until light and fluffy. Beat in egg. Stir in almonds.

Sift together dry ingredients and add to butter mixture along with sherry and extract. Mix until well combined and a dough is formed.

Roll out the dough on a well-floured board to $^1/_4$ inch thick. Cut out stars and place 1 inch apart on prepared baking sheet. Bake 10 to 12 minutes, or until cookies are lightly browned.

MAKES 4 TO 5 DOZEN COOKIES

Linzer Cookies

Most people can eat only one of these large, rich cookies. However, the combination of jam, nuts, and spices is so delectable that some may try to eat a second.

1   cup hazelnuts
1   cup unsalted butter, at
    room temperature
$^1/_2$ cup granulated sugar
$^1/_2$ cup confectioners' sugar
1   teaspoon vanilla

2   cups all-purpose flour
1   teaspoon cinnamon
$^1/_2$ teaspoon allspice
$^1/_4$ teaspoon cloves
$1^1/_2$ to 2 cups raspberry preserves
    Confectioners' sugar for sprinkling

A day or several hours before making the cookies, place hazelnuts in an ovenproof dish or pan in a 400°F oven for 15 to 20 minutes, or until the hazelnuts become golden; be careful not to let the nuts burn. Remove pan from oven and pour the hazelnuts onto a kitchen towel. Fold towel over nuts, making a package, and let nuts steam 2 to 3 minutes. Place your hand on the towel and make a circular motion, rubbing the hazelnuts against the fabric and the other nuts. After 2 to 3 minutes open the towel. Much of the skin from the hazelnuts will have fallen off. Don't worry if all the skin doesn't come completely off; there is usually some residue. Pick nuts out and allow them to cool completely. Finely grind the nuts in a coffee grinder or food processor.

Preheat oven to 375°F. Lightly coat baking sheets with cooking spray.

Place butter and sugars in a medium mixing bowl. Cream until light and fluffy. Beat in vanilla. Sift flour and spices together. Add to butter mix in three parts and blend well. Fold in nuts until thoroughly combined.

Pat out a third of the dough on a well-floured surface and roll out $1/4$ inch thick. Cut circles from dough with a $2^{1}/_{2}$-inch cookie cutter. Half the circles will be the tops and half will be bottoms. Cut a circle out of each of the tops. Place the circles 1 inch apart on a prepared baking sheet and bake 12 to 15 minutes, or until the circles begin to brown. Take the pan from the oven, leaving the cookies on the baking sheet.

Place preserves in a small pan over medium heat and cook until it boils and the jam becomes liquid. Spoon a generous teaspoon of preserves over each of the bottoms. Place tops over bottoms with a gentle swirling motion that will push the excess jam up through the center. Cool on a rack. Sprinkle on confectioners' sugar.

MAKES $1^{1}/_{2}$ TO 2 DOZEN
COOKIES

Macadamia Petites

Inspired by the cookies one finds in Belgium, these little wonders are both delicate and delectable.

$^1/_2$ cup unsalted butter, at
   room temperature
1 cup sifted confectioners' sugar
$^1/_2$ teaspoon vanilla
1 cup all-purpose flour

$^1/_2$ cup finely ground macadamia nuts
$^1/_2$ teaspoon baking powder
4 to 6 ounces high quality bittersweet
   chocolate, melted and cooled to
   room temperature

Cream butter and sugar until light and fluffy. Beat in vanilla. Add flour, nuts, and baking power, mixing well. Wrap dough in wax paper or plastic wrap and chill for 1 hour.

Preheat oven to 375°F. Line baking sheets with parchment paper.

Pat out half the dough on a lightly floured surface. Roll the dough to no more than $^1/_8$ inch thick. Using a 1- to 2-inch cookie cutter, cut small circles out of dough and place $^1/_2$ inch apart on a prepared baking sheet. Bake 10 to 12 minutes, or until cookies are lightly browned. Cool completely on a rack.

Carefully spread $^1/_2$ to 1 teaspoon melted chocolate on the flat side of a cookie and cover with a second cookie, flat side down. Continue making "sandwiches" with the remaining cookies. Let sandwiches sit until chocolate sets. If you're in a hurry, set them in the refrigerator for 15 minutes.

MAKES APPROXIMATELY 24 SANDWICHES

Sugar Cookie Christmas Balls

Sugar cookies are a traditional and delicious treat that are as much fun to make as they are to eat. Try this version with the children.

$^1/_2$ cup margarine
1 cup sugar
1 egg, beaten
1 teaspoon vanilla
2 cups all-purpose flour
$^1/_2$ teaspoon nutmeg
$^1/_2$ teaspoon baking powder

$^1/_2$ teaspoon salt
$^1/_2$ cup sour cream mixed with
    $^1/_2$ teaspoon baking soda
2 egg yolks
Red and green food coloring
Colored sugar crystals, optional
Silver dragées, optional

Cream margarine and sugar. Beat in egg and vanilla. Sift together dry ingredients and add to margarine and sugar mixture, one half at a time, alternating with the sour cream mixture, mixing until all ingredients are well combined and a dough is formed. Cover bowl with wax paper or plastic wrap and refrigerate for 2 hours.

Just before taking the dough out of the refrigerator, put each of the yolks in it's own small bowl and beat slightly. Add green food coloring to one bowl and red to the other. Mix well.

Preheat oven to 375°F. Grease baking sheets.

Pat out a third of the dough on a well-floured surface. Sprinkle a small amount of flour over the dough and roll it out $^1/_4$ inch thick. Cut out the cookies with a 2-inch cookie cutter and place on a prepared baking sheet 1 inch apart. Using a narrow pastry brush, paint half the circle red and the other half green. Should the dye mix become too thick, beat in $^1/_2$ teaspoon water. If desired, sprinkle colored sugar crystals over the cookies or decorate with silver dragées.

Bake 10 to 15 minutes, or until cookies are lightly browned on the bottom. Cool on a rack. Repeat this procedure until all the dough is used. Replenish the dye bowls with additional egg yolks as necessary.

MAKES APPROXIMATELY 2 DOZEN COOKIES

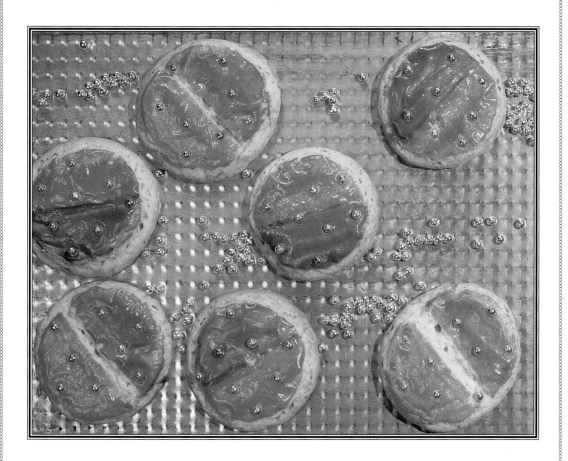

Pumpkin Drop Cookies

Even your favorite "cookie monster" will love these delicious, nutritious cookies.

Pumpkin Drop Cookies

$^1/_2$ cup butter or margarine

1 cup sugar

1 egg

1 cup canned pumpkin

1 teaspoon vanilla

2 cups all-purpose flour

1 teaspoon baking soda

$^3/_4$ teaspoon cinnamon

$^1/_4$ teaspoon salt

$^1/_4$ teaspoon nutmeg

1 cup raisins

1 cup chopped pecans or walnuts

Frosting

2 cups confectioners' sugar

2 tablespoons butter or margarine, softened

3 tablespoons finely shredded orange peel

2 tablespoons orange juice

Preheat oven to 375°F. Grease baking sheets.

In a large bowl, cream together butter or margarine and sugar until light and fluffy. Add egg, pumpkin, and vanilla and mix well.

In a medium bowl, stir together flour, baking soda, cinnamon, salt, and nutmeg. Add gradually to the pumpkin mixture and stir until blended. Stir in raisins and nuts.

Drop dough by rounded teaspoonfuls onto the baking sheets. Bake 12 to 15 minutes, or until lightly browned. Transfer to wire racks to cool completely. Mix frosting ingredients together, setting aside 1 tablespoon of shredded orange peel, and spread on cookies. Garnish with additional shredded orange peel.

MAKES 4 DOZEN COOKIES

Chocolate Chunk Macadamia Nut Cookies

Rich, chewy cookies bursting with nuts and chunks of chocolate are an appreciated treat any time of year.

$^1/_2$ cup unsalted butter, at
    room temperature

$^1/_2$ cup shortening

$^3/_4$ cup granulated sugar

$^3/_4$ cup packed light brown sugar

1 egg, beaten

2 teaspoons vanilla

$2^1/_2$ cups sifted all-purpose flour

1 teaspoon baking soda

$1^1/_4$ cups chocolate chunks

$^3/_4$ cup macadamia nuts, halved

Preheat oven to 375°F. Do not grease baking sheets.

    In a large mixing bowl, cream butter, shortening, and sugars until light and fluffy. Beat in egg and vanilla. Add flour and baking soda. Fold in chocolate chunks and macadamia nuts and blend until thoroughly mixed throughout the dough.

    Drop large rounded tablespoonfuls of the dough 3 inches apart onto ungreased baking sheets. Press down lightly on the top of each cookie and bake 10 to 12 minutes, or until lightly browned. Cool on wire racks.

MAKES $1^1/_2$ TO 2 DOZEN COOKIES

Nathaniel's Iced Banana Nut Cookies

These light, cakey cookies taste very much like banana nut bread—only crisper.

Banana Nut Cookies

1 cup sugar

¹/₂ cup shortening

1 teaspoon vanilla

2 cups sifted all-purpose flour

1 teaspoon baking powder

1 teaspoon cinnamon

¹/₂ teaspoon allspice

¹/₄ teaspoon salt

1 cup peeled and mashed ripe bananas

1 cup walnuts, toasted and coarsely chopped

1¹/₂ tablespoons unsalted butter, at room temperature

1¹/₂ cups confectioners' sugar

Icing

³/₄ teaspoon vanilla

1¹/₂ tablespoons hot water

Preheat oven to 375°F. Lightly coat baking sheets with cooking spray.

Cream sugar and shortening in a mixing bowl until light. Add vanilla. Sift together dry ingredients and add to the bowl with the shortening and mix well. Beat in bananas and nuts. Using a cookie scoop or a tablespoon, drop rounded amounts of dough 1 inch apart onto a prepared baking sheet. Bake 15 minutes, or until bottoms are very brown and the tops are lightly so. Using a spatula, remove cookies from baking sheet and place on wire racks. Cool completely.

Meanwhile, make the icing. Cream butter and sugar. Add vanilla and hot water, beating until a fine, drizzling consistency is achieved. If the icing is too thick, add additional hot water, ¹/₄ teaspoon at a time. Spread ¹/₂ to ³/₄ teaspoon of icing over the top of each cookie and let it drip down the sides. Let the cookies sit until the icing sets.

MAKES 2¹/₂ TO 3 DOZEN COOKIES

Especially Chocolate Cookies

These were made for a chocoholic friend who requested I make a cookie for her that had as much chocolate in it as possible. I added the almonds and used raspberry-flavored chocolate chips as a counterpoint to the chocolate, thus punching up the flavor.

1 cup unsalted butter, at room temperature
1½ cups granulated sugar
1½ cups packed dark brown sugar
2 eggs, beaten
1 teaspoon vanilla
2 ounces unsweetened chocolate, melted and cooled to room temperature

2½ cups sifted all-purpose flour
¼ cup unsweetened cocoa
1 teaspoon baking soda
½ teaspoon salt
1 cup chocolate chunks
1 cup raspberry-flavored chocolate chips
1 cup slivered almonds, toasted

Preheat oven to 375°F. Lightly grease baking sheets with cooking spray.

Cream butter and sugars until light and fluffy. Add eggs and vanilla. Beat in chocolate. Combine flour, cocoa, baking soda, and salt and add to the creamed mixture, half at a time, blending until thoroughly combined. Fold in chocolate chunks, chips, and almonds. Place heaping tablespoonfuls of dough 3 inches apart onto a prepared baking sheet. Bake 12 to 14 minutes. You will be able to smell these cookies as they approach doneness. Let the cookies remain on the baking sheet for 5 minutes, then place on wire racks to cool completely.

MAKES 2 TO 2½ DOZEN VERY LARGE COOKIES

Oatmeal Raisin Cookies

These lovely soft cookies are even better when served with ice-cold glasses of milk.

1 cup margarine at room temperature	1 teaspoon baking soda
1 cup sugar	$^1/_2$ teaspoon salt
2 eggs, beaten	$^1/_2$ cup milk
1 teaspoon vanilla	2 cups uncooked oatmeal
2 cups sifted all-purpose flour	$1^1/_2$ cups raisins
1 teaspoon baking powder	$1^1/_2$ cups walnut pieces, optional

Preheat oven to 375°F. Lightly grease baking sheets.

Cream margarine and sugar until light and fluffy. Mix in eggs and vanilla. Combine flour, baking powder, baking soda, and salt. Add to the creamed mix, half at a time, along with the milk. Blend in oatmeal, raisins, and walnuts. Spoon heaping tablespoonfuls 2 inches apart onto a prepared baking sheet. Bake 12 to 15 minutes, or until cookies are browned. Cool on a wire rack.

Variation: Add 1 cup peanut butter chips to the batter.

MAKES $1^1/_2$ TO 2 DOZEN LARGE COOKIES

Mexican Chocolate Sugar Cookies

Crisp and sugary on the outside, these rich chocolate treats have a hint of cinnamon and a chewy inside texture. These cookies are hardy, and mail well.

³/₄	cup shortening		1³/₄	cups all-purpose flour
1	cup sugar		2	teaspoons baking soda
1	egg		1	teaspoon cinnamon
¹/₄	cup light corn syrup		¹/₄	teaspoon salt
2	ounces unsweetened chocolate, melted and cooled to room temperature		1	cup semisweet chocolate pieces
			¹/₄	cup sugar, for coating

Preheat oven to 350°F. Lightly grease baking sheets.

In a large bowl, cream together shortening, 1 cup sugar, and egg with an electric mixer. Stir in corn syrup and unsweetened chocolate. In a small bowl, stir together the flour, baking soda, cinnamon, and salt. Stir into shortening mixture to make a stiff dough. Add chocolate pieces and mix to incorporate. Pour ¹/₄ cup sugar into another small bowl, or onto a saucer. Shape the dough into 1-inch balls, and roll each ball in sugar. Place on prepared baking sheet, 2 inches apart, and bake 10 minutes, or until cookies are puffed and the tops crack. Let cookies cool for a few minutes before removing to a wire rack to cool completely.

MAKES ABOUT 4 DOZEN COOKIES

German Fruity Spritzes

Colorful jams make these spritz bars glisten like stained glass. Their festive hues will brighten any gift box or cookie tray.

1 cup butter, softened	$2^2/_3$ cups flour
$^1/_2$ cup packed brown sugar	1 teaspoon baking powder
1 egg	2 cups strawberry or pineapple jam
1 teaspoon vanilla	

Preheat oven to 400°F. Do not grease baking sheets.

Cream together butter and brown sugar, then add egg and vanilla and stir to incorporate. Sift flour and baking powder together, then gradually stir them into the creamed ingredients until thoroughly mixed.

Put half the dough into a cookie press with a 1-inch ribbon plate. Press out 10 strips, each 10 inches long, onto ungreased baking sheets. Now change the plate to a star decorator's tip, and, using the rest of the dough, form 2 rims along the sides of each of the 10 ribbons, piping a dough rim on top of the existing dough. Carefully spoon jam down the center of each of the strips.

Bake 8 to 10 minutes. While cookies are still hot, cut strips on the diagonal $1^1/_4$ inches wide, then let cool.

MAKES ABOUT 4 DOZEN COOKIES

Galettes

This is my take on the wonderfully rich butter cookies from the Breton region of France.

2 cups unsalted butter, at room temperature

1 cup granulated sugar

1 teaspoon vanilla

$^1/_2$ teaspoon almond extract

3 cups sifted all-purpose flour

1 teaspoon baking powder

About 4 tablespoons butter, melted

Turbinado sugar for sprinkling

Cream butter and sugar until light and fluffy. Beat in vanilla and almond extract. Mix in flour and baking powder until well combined. Lay a sheet of wax paper onto a smooth surface. Spoon half the dough onto the wax paper. Lightly flour your hands and form two rolls, each approximately 9 inches long and 2 inches in diameter, out of the sticky dough. Wrap each roll in wax paper, twisting ends of the paper, and refrigerate 2 to 3 hours.

Preheat oven to 400°F. Do no grease baking sheets.

Take dough out of the refrigerator and cut the rolls into $^1/_4$-inch slices. Place slices 2 inches apart on an ungreased baking sheet. Using a pastry brush, lightly coat top of each cookie with melted butter and sprinkle with sugar. Bake 12 to 14 minutes, or until cookies are nicely browned. Cool on a rack.

MAKES 4 TO 5 DOZEN COOKIES

Black-Eyed Susans

These flower-shaped cookies with chocolate centers remind me of the bloom for which they're named.

1 cup unsalted butter, at
   room temperature
³/₄ cup sugar
1 teaspoon vanilla

2¹/₂ cups sifted all-purpose flour
1 teaspoon baking powder
About ¹/₂ cup mini-chocolate chips

Preheat oven to 375°F. Line baking sheets with parchment paper.

Cream butter and sugar until light and fluffy. Beat in vanilla. Mix in flour and baking powder until thoroughly combined. Fill a cookie press fitted with a flower plate with dough and press flowers 1 inch apart onto a prepared baking sheet. Bake 12 to 14 minutes, or until cookies are lightly browned. Remove pan from oven. Leaving cookies on pan, fill center of each with mini-chocolate chips. Wait a minute or two and then, using the tip of a sharp knife, smooth centers. Let cookies remain on pan for an additional 5 minutes, then place on a wire rack to cool completely.

MAKES 4 TO 5 DOZEN COOKIES

Buttery Spritz Cookies

These Christmas classics can be made in many shapes and sizes. Shape them with a cookie press or cookie "gun," or put the dough in a pastry bag and force it through a wide pastry tip. Decorate with colored sprinkles, candied cherries, or a dusting of sugar.

1 cup butter

$^2/_3$ cup sugar

2 egg yolks

1 teaspoon vanilla

2 cups all-purpose flour

Colored sprinkles or sugar, optional

Candied cherries, halved or cut up, optional

Preheat oven to 375°F. Do not grease baking sheets.

In a large bowl, cream butter until light and fluffy. Add sugar gradually and continue beating until fluffy. Add egg yolks and vanilla and beat well. Mix in flour by hand until just blended; do not overmix.

Spoon mixture into a cookie press or cookie gun and press cookies in star, tree, wreath, or bar shapes onto ungreased baking sheets. Or use a pastry bag fitted with a wide star or round tip to form wreaths, canes, or pretzels. Decorate with colored sprinkles or sugar, or press candied cherries into cookies.

Bake 8 to 10 minutes, or until just firm, but not brown. Remove to wire racks to cool completely.

Variations: For almond spritz, add $^1/_2$ teaspoon almond extract with the vanilla. Sprinkle with finely chopped (not ground) toasted almonds before baking. For orange spritz, add 2 teaspoons finely shredded orange peel with the vanilla.

MAKES 3½ TO 5 DOZEN COOKIES

Almond Slices

Simple ingredients are the secret behind this delicious sliced cookie. The dough can be made well in advance, and sliced and baked just when you want it.

1   cup unsalted butter, at
    room temperature
$^1/_2$ cup granulated sugar
$^1/_2$ cup packed light brown sugar
1   egg, beaten
1   teaspoon vanilla

$^3/_4$ teaspoon almond extract
$2^1/_2$ cups sifted all-purpose flour
1   teaspoon baking soda
$^1/_2$ teaspoon cinnamon
1   cup slivered almonds, toasted

Cream butter and sugars until light and fluffy. Add egg and extract. Mix in flour, baking soda, and cinnamon. Fold in almonds. Divide dough in half, placing each half on a sheet of wax paper. Flour your hands and shape each piece into a roll approximately 10 × 2 inches. Wrap each roll in wax paper and refrigerate overnight.

Preheat oven to 375°F. Lightly grease baking sheets with cooking spray.

Remove rolls from the refrigerator and unwrap, one at a time, and cut into $^1/_4$-inch slices. Place the slices 1 inch apart on a prepared baking sheet and bake 12 to 14 minutes, or until lightly browned. Cool on wire racks.

MAKES APPROXIMATELY 4 DOZEN COOKIES

Horseshoes

The Italian name for these butter cookies is *crumiri*. Slightly sweet, slightly crunchy, these cookies are wonderful with both cappuccino and American brewed coffee.

1 cup unsalted butter, at room temperature
$^2/_3$ cup sugar
2 large eggs, beaten

$1^1/_2$ cups all-purpose flour
1 cup fine yellow cornmeal
$^1/_4$ teaspoon baking powder
$^1/_4$ teaspoon salt

Preheat oven to 325°F. Line baking sheets with parchment paper.

Cream butter and sugar until light and fluffy. Beat in eggs. Add dry ingredients and mix until a smooth dough is formed. Fill a cookie press or pastry bag with dough and pipe small horseshoe shapes onto a prepared baking sheet. You should use no more than 2 to 3 inches of dough to create these ridged rounded shapes. Bake 15 to 20 minutes, or until cookies are lightly browned. Let sit in pan for 5 minutes before transferring to a wire rack to cool completely.

Variation: Stud each horseshoe with pignoli nuts before baking for an even crunchier cookie.

MAKES 3 TO 4 DOZEN COOKIES

Pecan Crescents

A traditional Christmas treat for many families, these tender butter cookies can be enjoyed year-round.

1 cup butter, softened
¹/₄ cup confectioners' sugar
1 tablespoon water
1 teaspoon vanilla

2 cups all-purpose flour
2 cups very finely chopped pecans
Confectioners' sugar, for coating

Preheat oven to 325°F. Do not grease baking sheets.

In a large bowl, cream butter until fluffy and white. Gradually add ¹/₄ cup sugar, then beat in water and vanilla until fluffy. By hand, stir in flour and pecans. Cover and chill for at least 1 hour. (The dough will be a little sticky.)

Using about 1 tablespoon dough for each cookie, form small logs, each about 3 inches long. Bend each log into a crescent shape. Place on an ungreased baking sheet and bake 20 minutes, or until very lightly browned.

Put some confectioners' sugar in a bowl, and roll the hot cookies in it. Place on a wire rack to cool completely.

Variation: To make smaller cookies, use about 1 teaspoon dough to form 1-inch crescents. Bake for about 15 minutes. Making them this size yields about 12 dozen.

MAKES ABOUT 4 DOZEN COOKIES

Cinnamon Stars

These spicy butter cookies will simply melt in your mouth.

1^1/$_4$ cups butter, softened

^{3}/$_4$ cup confectioners' sugar

2^1/$_2$ cups all-purpose flour

2   teaspoons cinnamon

^{1}/$_2$ teaspoon nutmeg

1 teaspoon vanilla

Confectioners' sugar for sprinkling

In a large bowl, cream butter. Gradually add ^{3}/$_4$ cup confectioners' sugar and beat until light and fluffy. In another bowl, stir together flour, cinnamon, and nutmeg. Add dry ingredients to creamed mixture. Stir in vanilla and mix well. Divide into four equal portions. Cover and chill at least 1 hour.

Preheat oven to 325°F. Do not grease baking sheets.

On a lightly floured surface, roll out one portion of the dough at a time, ^{1}/$_4$ inch thick. Cut out with a 1- or 2-inch star-shaped cookie cutter, dipping the cutter in flour as needed to keep dough from sticking. Place cookies on an ungreased baking sheet and bake 12 to 15 minutes for 1-inch cookies, 15 to 18 minutes for 2-inch cookies. Remove to a wire rack to cool. Sprinkle cookies with confectioners' sugar.

MAKES 5 TO 10 DOZEN, DEPENDING ON SIZE

Strawberry Crumble Bars

Bright red strawberry preserves give these crumble bars a festive look. They make a perfect treat for afternoon teas and parties.

Crust

$^3/_4$ cup unsalted butter, at
    room temperature

$^1/_2$ cup confectioners' sugar

$1^1/_2$ cups sifted all-purpose flour

Crumble

1   cup sifted all-purpose flour

$1^1/_2$ cups sugar

$^1/_2$ cup chilled butter, cut into pieces

3 cups flaked coconut

$^3/_4$ cup strawberry preserves

Preheat oven to 350°F. Grease a 9-inch square pan.

Combine crust ingredients and, using the paddle attachment for a mixer or a pastry cutter, work ingredients just to the point where a smooth dough is formed. Press the dough evenly into the bottom of the prepared pan. Bake 15 to 18 minutes, or until the edges begin to brown.

While the crust is baking, prepare the crumble by mixing flour and sugar. Cut in butter until mix is crumbly and has small peanut-size pieces. Toss in coconut, mixing well.

Remove crust from oven. Spread preserves over the hot crust. Sprinkle crumble evenly over preserves. Press down lightly. Bake 35 to 45 minutes, or until coconut has browned and top of crumble feels set. Cool completely and cut into bar sizes of your choice.

MAKES 9 TO 18 BARS, DEPENDING ON SIZE

Glazed Lemon Bars

These classic, tart lemon squares are an enduring favorite.

Pastry

³/₄ cup unsalted butter, at room temperature

¹/₂ cup sifted confectioners' sugar

1¹/₂ cups sifted all-purpose flour

Filling

2 eggs plus 1 egg yolk, slightly beaten

1 cup granulated sugar

3 tablespoons fresh lemon juice

Grated zest of 1 lemon

Glaze

1 cup sifted confectioners' sugar

2 teaspoons fresh lemon juice

Water as needed

Preheat oven to 350°F. Grease a 9-inch square pan.

Using the paddle attachment of your mixer (or a pastry cutter, if you prefer to do it by hand), combine all the pastry ingredients and mix only until a smooth dough is formed. Press dough into bottom of the prepared pan. Bake 15 to 18 minutes, or until edges of the crust are lightly browned.

While crust is baking, whisk together ingredients for filling. Remove crust from oven and pour filling evenly over crust. Bake 25 to 30 minutes, or until filling is set and beginning to brown. Remove from oven and cool for 20 minutes.

Prepare glaze by beating together confectioners' sugar and lemon juice. Add enough water, 1 teaspoon at a time, to make a spreadable glaze. Carefully spoon glaze over filling, making sure it is entirely covered. Let sit until completely cool. Cut into bar sizes of your choice.

Variation: Place a candied violet in the center of each bar, pressing down slightly so the flowers stick to the glaze and don't fall off.

MAKES 9 TO 18 BARS, DEPENDING ON SIZE.

Raspberry Coconut Bars

These tasty, tender bars make a great after-school treat for kids and parents alike.

Dough

¹/₂ cup unsalted butter, at
    room temperature

¹/₂ cup granulated sugar
1¹/₂ cups sifted all-purpose flour

Topping

²/₃ cup packed light brown sugar
¹/₂ cup sifted all-purpose flour
6 tablespoons chilled unsalted butter

1 cup flaked coconut
¹/₂ cup coarsely chopped pecans
¹/₂ cup mini chocolate chips

Filling

³/₄ cup raspberry preserves

Preheat oven to 375°F. Lightly grease a 9-inch square pan.

Cream butter and sugar. Add flour and mix until thoroughly combined. Press the dough firmly into the prepared pan. Bake 20 minutes, or until crust begins to brown.

While dough is baking, prepare topping by combining sugar and flour. Cut butter into sugar and flour until a crumbly mixture is formed. Toss in coconut, pecans, and chocolate chips, mixing well.

Remove dough from oven. Carefully spread the preserves over crust. Spoon topping mixture over preserves, distributing it evenly. Press down firmly and return to oven for an additional 30 minutes. When done, top should be browned and firm. Cool and cut into bar sizes of your choice.

MAKES 9 TO 18 BARS, DEPENDING ON SIZE

Pecan Wedges

Rich and nutty, these delicious pecan wedges are even tastier when dipped in chocolate.

Crust

³/₄ cup unsalted butter, at room temperature

¹/₄ cup shortening

³/₄ cup confectioners' sugar

2 cups sifted all-purpose flour

Pecan Praline

1 cup dark brown sugar

1 egg

1¹/₂ tablespoons all-purpose flour

1 tablespoon vanilla

2 cups pecans

About 8 ounces good quality milk, semisweet or bittersweet chocolate

Preheat oven to 375°F. Lightly grease a 9 × 13-inch pan.

Prepare crust by creaming butter, shortening, and sugar. Beat in flour, mixing until ingredients are thoroughly combined and a dough is formed. Press dough into the bottom of the prepared pan. Push dough slightly (about 1 inch) up the sides of the pan. Bake 10 minutes.

While crust is baking, prepare praline by beating together brown sugar, egg, flour, and vanilla. Mix in pecans and stir until all the nuts are coated. Remove crust from oven. Pour pecan praline over the crust, spreading evenly, but leaving 1 inch around the edge of the crust uncovered. Bake 20 minutes, or until praline has set and crust has browned. Remove from oven and cool completely.

Melt chocolate in top of a double boiler. Pour into a bowl and set aside. Using a sharp knife, make a cut in the exact center of the pan down its entire length. Going down each side, cut the praline on the horizontal into bars. The bars can be 1, 1¹/₂, or 2 inches wide, depending on your preference. The end result will be bars approximately 4¹/₂ inches in length, with a section of header crust on one end. Tilt the bowl of chocolate so that a deep pool is formed. With a firm grip, carefully dip each bar, crust side down, into the chocolate as far is it will go. Remove bar and place it on a sheet of wax paper. When all the bars have been dipped, let them remain on the wax paper until chocolate has dried and set.

MAKES 12 TO 24 BARS, DEPENDING ON SIZE

Black and White "Pretzels"

Children will love these twisty, delicious cookies.

1 cup plus 2 tablespoons unsalted butter, at room temperature

1 cup sifted confectioners' sugar

1 egg, beaten

1 teaspoon vanilla

1 1/2 cups sifted all-purpose flour

About 8 ounces bittersweet chocolate

Cream the 1 cup butter and sugar. Add egg and vanilla. Mix in flour. Spoon dough onto wax paper and wrap it. Refrigerate 1 to 2 hours, or until dough has stiffened.

Preheat oven to 375°F. Lightly grease baking sheets.

Remove a third of the dough, keeping the rest refrigerated until you need it. Flour your hands and pinch off enough dough to make a small ball. Using the palm of your hand, roll the ball into a thin tube approximately 8 × 10 × 1/4 inches. Form the tubes into the shape of pretzels and place them 1 inch apart on a prepared baking sheet. Bake 12 to 15 minutes, or until lightly browned. Cool on a wire rack.

Melt chocolate and remaining 2 tablespoons butter in the top of a double boiler, stirring until smooth. Cover a plate or baking sheet with wax paper. Dip half of each pretzel in the chocolate and place on wax paper to set. To speed up the process, refrigerate the cookies until the chocolate has stiffened.

MAKES 2½ TO 3 DOZEN "PRETZELS"

Elizabeth Newkirk's Coconut Macaroons

Macaroons are flourless cookies traditionally served in Jewish homes during Passover. Their festive look and timeless sweet flavor make them a great cookie for any holiday, any time of year.

$2^2/_3$ cups packed flaked coconut
1 cup sweetened condensed milk
2 teaspoons vanilla

$^3/_4$ teaspoon almond extract
$^1/_4$ teaspoon salt

Preheat oven to 350°F. Heavily grease baking sheets.

Combine all ingredients in a mixing bowl, blending until all the coconut is wet and the condensed milk is completely absorbed. Spoon rounded teaspoonfuls onto a prepared baking sheet 1 to $1^1/_2$ inches apart. Slightly shape cookies into mounds with your fingers. Bake 10 to 12 minutes, or until browned on the bottom and slightly brown on top. Let cookies remain on pan before placing them on wire racks to cool completely.

MAKES APPROXIMATELY $1^1/_2$ TO 2 DOZEN MACAROONS

Wiggy's Chocolate Mocha Cookies

These tasty sandwich cookies can be refrigerated for up to a week. Although they may be taken out of the fridge 1 hour before serving, they are fabulous cold!

Cookies

1 cup unsalted butter, at room temperature	2 ounces unsweetened chocolate, melted and cooled to room temperature
3 ounces cream cheese, softened	1 teaspoon vanilla
1 cup granulated sugar	$2^{1}/_{2}$ cups sifted all-purpose flour
1 egg, beaten	1 teaspoon baking powder

Ganache Filling

6 ounces bitter or semisweet chocolate	$^{1}/_{2}$ cup unsalted butter, at room temperature
2 teaspoons powdered espresso	
$^{1}/_{2}$ cup heavy cream	2 cups sifted confectioners' sugar

Cream butter and cream cheese. Beat in sugar until light and fluffy. Blend in egg, chocolate, and vanilla. Add flour and baking powder, mixing well. Cover dough and chill $^{1}/_{2}$ hour.

Preheat oven to 350°F. Do not grease baking sheets.

Fill the cookie press using a swirl plate and press swirls $^{1}/_{2}$ inch apart directly onto an ungreased baking sheet. Bake 10 minutes. Let cookies sit on baking sheet for 5 minutes. Cool on wire racks.

While cookies are cooling, prepare filling. Break chocolate into the bowl of a food processor fitted with the metal blade. Add the espresso and pulse until the chocolate is finely ground. (This can also be done by shaving the chocolate using a very sharp knife, but it is time-consuming.) Pour chocolate into a bowl. Heat cream just until boiling and pour over chocolate. Stir chocolate and cream until thick and smooth. Beat in butter until well combined. Add confectioners' sugar, mixing until a smooth filling is achieved.

Spread a full teaspoon of filling over the flat side of a cookie. Top with the flat side of a second cookie. Continue until all the cookies have been made into sandwiches. Let sit until filling sets.

MAKES 2½ TO 3 DOZEN SANDWICHES

Alice's Date Filled Cookies

You can substitute your favorite jam or jelly for the date filling in this recipe.

1 cup chopped dates

$^1/_2$ cup water

1 tablespoon fresh lemon juice

$^1/_2$ cup chopped walnuts, optional

2 cups sifted all-purpose flour

1 cup packed light brown sugar

$^1/_2$ cup unsalted butter, at room temperature

1 egg, beaten

1 teaspoon vanilla

1 teaspoon baking soda

$^1/_3$ cup milk

Sifted confectioners' sugar for sprinkling

Combine dates, water, and lemon juice in a small saucepan and cook over a low heat until water is absorbed. Remove pan from heat and stir in walnuts if desired. Cool.

Mix together flour and brown sugar. Cut in butter. Combine egg and vanilla. Dissolve baking soda in milk. Add the two liquids to flour mixture half at a time. Blend until thoroughly combined. Cover and chill dough for at least 1 hour, or until it has stiffened and is workable.

Preheat oven to 375°F. Lightly grease baking sheets.

Place a third of the dough on a well-floured surface. Sprinkle a small amount of flour over the top of the dough and roll out $^1/_4$ inch thick. Cut out circles with a $2^1/_2$-inch cookie cutter. Spoon $^1/_2$ to 1 teaspoon of the date mixture into the center of each circle. Fold circle over so that the ends meet to form a half-moon shape. Press edges together and place 1 inch apart on a prepared baking sheet. Bake 12 to 15 minutes, or until cookies are browned. Cool on a wire rack and sprinkle lightly with confectioners' sugar.

MAKES ABOUT 2 DOZEN COOKIES

Chinese Almond Cookies

These are a small version of those wonderful crispy cookies served at the end of a meal in Chinese restaurants.

1 cup shortening
$^1/_2$ cup sugar
$^1/_2$ teaspoon almond extract
$1^1/_2$ cups all-purpose flour
$^1/_2$ cup finely ground blanched almonds

$^1/_2$ teaspoon baking powder
1 egg yolk mixed with 1 tablespoon cold water
Whole blanched almonds

Preheat the oven to 400°F. Lightly grease baking sheets.

Cream shortening and sugar until light and fluffy. Add extract. Blend in flour, ground almonds, and baking powder. Mix well. Divide dough in half. Place half the dough on a sheet of wax paper. Lightly flour your hands and shape dough into a 10 × 2-inch log. Wrap log in wax paper and refrigerate for at least 1 hour. Shape the remaining dough into a second log. Turn logs from time to time as they sit in the refrigerator to avoid a flat side.

Remove logs from refrigerator. Cut into $^1/_2$-inch slices and place on a prepared baking sheet 1 inch apart. Brush tops of the cookies lightly with the egg yolk mixture. Press a whole blanched almond in the center of each cookie. Bake 10 to 13 minutes, or until cookies are browned. Remove pan from oven and allow to sit for 10 minutes before placing them on a wire rack to cool completely.

MAKES 2$^1/_2$ TO 3 DOZEN COOKIES

Peanut Blossoms

These peanut butter cookies with a chocolate kiss in the center have been a favorite of children of all ages for decades.

$^1/_2$ cup shortening

$^1/_2$ cup packed light brown sugar

$^1/_2$ cup granulated sugar

$^3/_4$ cup peanut butter, crunchy or smooth

1   egg, beaten

2   teaspoons vanilla

$1^3/_4$ cups all-purpose flour

1   teaspoon baking soda

$^1/_2$ teaspoon salt

$^1/_4$ to $^1/_2$ cup granulated sugar for rolling

About 3 dozen chocolate kisses

Preheat oven to 375°F. Lightly grease baking sheets.

Cream shortening and sugars until light and fluffy. Mix in peanut butter. Beat in egg and vanilla. Mix in flour, baking soda, and salt, blending thoroughly until a dough is formed. Shape the dough into balls using approximately 1 full teaspoon dough for each. Roll each ball in granulated sugar and place 1 inch apart on a prepared baking sheet. Bake 10 minutes.

Remove pan from oven. Place a chocolate kiss in the center of each ball and press down gently until cookie begins to crack. Bake an additional 3 minutes. Allow cookies to sit on baking sheet for 3 minutes before placing them on wire racks to cool completely.

MAKES ABOUT 3 DOZEN COOKIES

Cranberry Almond Biscotti

These cranberry-flecked cookies are a festive version of traditional biscotti.

$^1/_2$ cup dried cranberries	1 egg yolk
$2^1/_2$ cups sifted all-purpose flour	4 tablespoons fresh orange juice
1 cup sugar	$^1/_2$ teaspoon vanilla
$1^1/_2$ teaspoons baking powder	$^1/_2$ teaspoon almond extract
$^1/_2$ teaspoon salt	1 cup slivered almonds, toasted
2 eggs	

Preheat oven to 350°F. Heavily grease baking sheet.

Shortly before beginning, boil water and pour just enough over cranberries to cover them and let sit until they plump. Drain.

Combine dry ingredients in a large bowl. Mix in eggs, yolk, juice, and flavorings, stirring until a dough is formed. (If you're using a mixer, a wide or paddle attachment would be best.) Fold in the cranberries and almonds.

Place dough on a well-floured surface and knead until dough is elastic and workable. If dough is very wet, sprinkle flour, a small amount at a time, over the dough and work it in.

Divide dough in half and shape each half into a 12 × 2-inch rectangular log. Place logs 4 to 5 inches apart on prepared baking sheet. Bake 30 minutes. Remove pan from oven and let logs sit 10 minutes.

Place each log on a smooth surface and slice into $^1/_2$-inch slices on the diagonal. Place the slices, wide side down, on the baking sheet and bake 12 to 15 minutes, or until undersides of the cookies are lightly browned. Turn cookies over and repeat the browning process for an additional 12 to 15 minutes. Cool on a wire rack.

MAKES $2^1/_2$ TO 3 DOZEN BISCOTTI

Patty's Peanut Butter Balls

My dear friend Patricia Shelly Bushman makes and shares these tasty treats every Christmas. Once you've tried them, they'll become one of your holiday traditions, too!

3 cups semisweet chocolate pieces
  (about 18 ounces)

2 tablespoons shortening

1 12-ounce jar chunky peanut butter

1 15-ounce package confectioners'
  sugar, sifted

$1^1/_2$ cups graham cracker crumbs

1 cup sweetened shredded coconut

1 cup butter or margarine, melted

In the top of a double boiler or in a microwave, melt chocolate and shortening together. Set aside and keep warm.

In a large bowl, mix together the peanut butter, sugar, cracker crumbs, and coconut. Pour butter or margarine over peanut butter mixture and mix well. Shape mixture into 1-inch balls. Use a fork to dip each ball into the chocolate, covering the candy completely, allowing excess chocolate to drain off. Place each ball on wax paper and leave until set, about 4 hours.

MAKES ABOUT 7 DOZEN COOKIES

U.S.–Metric Cooking Conversions

U.S	Metric
1/4 teaspoon	1.2 ml
1/2 teaspoon	2.5 ml
3/4 teaspoon	3.7 ml
1 teaspoon	4.9 ml
1 1/4 teaspoons	6.2 ml
1 1/2 teaspoons	7.4 ml
1 3/4 teaspoons	8.6 ml
2 teaspoons	9.9 ml
1 tablespoon	14.8 ml

U.S	Metric
2 tablespoons	29.6 ml
1/4 cup	59.2 ml
1/2 cup	118.3 ml
1 cup	236.6 ml
2 cups or 1 pint	473.2 ml
3 cups	709.8 ml
4 cups or 1 quart	946.4 ml
4 quarts or 1 gallon	3.8 liters

Fahrenheit	Celsius
32°	0°
40°	4.4°
50°	10°
60°	15.6°
70°	21.1°
80°	26.7°
90°	32.2°
100°	37.8°
110°	43.3°
120°	48.9°
130°	54.4°
140°	60°
150°	65.6°

Fahrenheit	Celsius
160°	71.1°
170°	76.7°
180°	82.2°
190°	87.8°
200°	93.3°
212°	100°
250°	121°
300°	149°
350°	177°
400°	205°
450°	233°
500°	260°

Index

Photo Credits

© Michael Grand: 11, 39
© Bill Milne: 16, 27, 36, 44, 51, 52, 61, 76
© Zeva Olbaum: 3, 4, 7, 9, 12, 13, 14, 15, 19, 21, 22, 25, 28, 31, 32, 35, 40, 43, 47, 48, 55, 57, 59, 61, 62, 64, 67, 68, 71, 72, 75